G000255256

SPIRIT OF THE

ISLE OF WIGHT STEAM RAILWAY

MIKE HEATH

First published in Great Britain in 2010

British Library Cataloguing-in-Publication Data
A CIP record for this title is available from the British Library

ISBN 978 0 85710 008 5

PiXZ Books
Halsgrove House, Ryelands Industrial Estate,
Bagley Road, Wellington, Somerset TA21 9PZ
Tel: 01823 653777
Fax: 01823 216796
email: sales@halsgrove.com

An imprint of Halstar Ltd, part of the Halsgrove group of companies
Information on all Halsgrove titles is available at: www.halsgrove.com

Printed and bound in China by Toppan Leefung Printing Ltd

Introduction

In the golden age of steam the Isle of Wight could boast an impressive 54 miles of railway. Opened in 1862, the line between Cowes and Newport was the first connection on the island and more branch lines followed. Next was the Isle of Wight Railway's linking of Ryde and Shanklin. The Newport Junction Railway ran across to Sandown and in 1875 a line was opened between Ryde and Newport. 1889 saw the Freshwater, Yarmouth and Newport Railway emerge to serve the west of the island with the final link from Merstone to Ventnor, via St. Lawrence, completed in 1900. For many years the railways were an important contributor to the island's economy and the variety of engines, carriages and wagons that worked on them, many bought second-hand from the mainland, gave it a charm much appreciated by visitors.

In 1923 all the lines became a part of the Southern Railway and the whole system was improved and modernised. The 1930s saw holiday traffic reach record levels and, excepting the war years, this trend continued into the early 1950s. As on the mainland, competition from road transport proved too much and as the 1960s dawned closure was proposed. By 1966 all that remained was the Ryde to Shanklin section and that same year saw the last steam train on that line.

However the trains that had remained on the island had attracted a devoted following and a group of enthusiasts collectively sought to save a locomotive and a few carriages for static exhibition. Initially their stock had been kept at the closed Newport Station but in 1971 all was relocated to Havenstreet and they commenced passenger services between there and Wootton. Daily running during the summer season started in the 1980s and the line was extended to Smallbrook, alongside the Ryde to Shanklin route, in 1991.

The Isle of Wight Steam Railway of today passes through five miles of totally unspoiled countryside and its rural charm has attracted both enthusiasts and holidaymakers for many years. With many of the society's locomotives and all of its carriages having spent much of their working lives on the island, the railway is a living, breathing museum. Truly a journey back in time.

One of the preserved locomotives that spent part of its working life on the island is A1/x Class 'Terrier' W8 *Freshwater*. Built in 1876 by the London, Brighton and South Coast Railway it was island based between 1913 and 1949. It was withdrawn by British Railways in 1963 and returned to the island, after a period of private ownership, in 1979.

The railway's other 'Terrier', W11 *Newport,* was built by the LBSCR in 1878 and exhibited at the Paris Exhibition that same year. It worked on the island from 1902 until 1947. Like *Freshwater* it was withdrawn in 1963 but placed on static display at Butlin's Pwllheli holiday camp. Its own island return was in 1973.

All the coaches preserved have seen regular service on the island since before the end of British Railways and the IOWSR is unique amongst preserved railways in Britain in running trains exclusively with traditional wooden compartment coaches. The Victorian era saw mainly 4 or 6 wheeler coaches providing passenger accommodation and the railway has several examples. No 4112 is a Third Class and Guard's Brake Van that dates from 1898. It arrived on the island in 1924 and was rebuilt at Havenstreet in 1991.

By the early 1900s longer carriages with a bogie at each end were being introduced and examples that worked on the Isle of Wight have also been preserved. Built in 1911 No. 6375 arrived on the island in 1949.

Our journey starts at Smallbrook Junction Station where the lines from Ryde to Ventnor and Ryde to Newport diverge. The platforms on each line are only accessible by rail and the station itself was only built in 1990–91. Visitors arriving by 'Island Line' electric train will have already ridden in heritage stock as that line operates former London Underground trains.

Freshwater attracts the attention of passengers as the guard advises of imminent departure.

The train passes through woodland on the climb away from Ashey Road Bridge, also known as Long Arch.

499
SOUTHERN
11
STEPNEY
2

Left:
In 2001 the railway held a 'Terrier Rail Gala' and their own examples of that class of locomotive were joined by two visitors from the Bluebell Railway in Sussex. One of which, No. 55 *Stepney,* pilots W11 *Newport* and the Edwardian bogie coaches on the climb heading east away from Ashey Station.

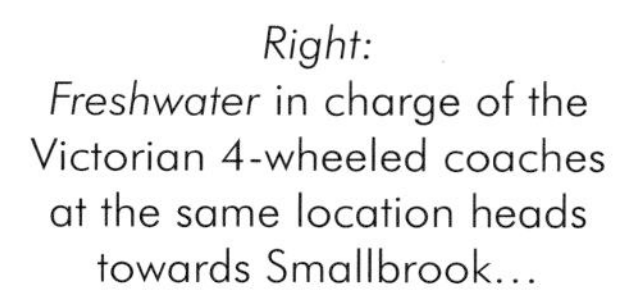

Right:
Freshwater in charge of the Victorian 4-wheeled coaches at the same location heads towards Smallbrook...

...returning a little later.

It is hard to believe but the station at Ashey once had two platforms and a loop. There was also a siding which branched off to Ashey Down. Ashey racecourse was alongside the siding and carriages used to be left there for use as grandstands on race days!

Leaving Ashey for Havenstreet is Hunslet 0-6-0ST WD198 *Royal Engineer*. Built in 1953 it entered Ministry of Defence (Army) service at Steventon in 1956 moving to Bicester two years later and on to Long Marston in 1961. It arrived on the island in 1992 initially on loan from the National Army Museum. Ownership transferred to the IOWSR in 2008.

Arriving at Ashey from Havenstreet is 02 Class 0-4-4T W24 *Calbourne*. Originally constructed in 1891 at the Nine Elms locomotive works of the London and South Western Railway, this was the last survivor of its class and the first engine acquired by the steam railway in 1967.

SOUTHERN
24

Left:
Seen here on the return journey, *Calbourne* was based at Fratton then Exeter in her early years with ownership passing to the Southern Railway in 1923. Two years later she was shipped to the island as part of the then modernisation programme.

Right:
In 2001, *Newport* was carrying the unlined black livery of the Southern Railway. The old Ashey Station House can just be seen in the trees behind the first carriage.

A panoramic view of a Smallbrook-bound train approaching the line's summit at Ashey. In the background, across the water is the 150-metre-high Spinnaker Tower the centrepiece of the redevelopment of Portsmouth Harbour.

Left:
A view from the train of the open countryside between Havenstreet and Ashey.

A view across the countryside of the train in exactly the same location!

Fenchurch and the predominantly Victorian stock catch the evening sunshine on the climb away from Havenstreet.

L.B. & S.C.R No. 672 *Fenchurch* visited for the 'Terrier Rail Gala' in 2001. Its usual base is the Bluebell Railway in Sussex where it has the distinction of being their oldest locomotive having been built in 1872.

Spring is still to show in this April 2007 view of *Freshwater* gliding into Havenstreet with a Wootton-bound service.

HAVEN STREET
SOUTHERN RAILWAY
REFRESHMENTS

Left:
The heart of the Isle of Wight Steam Railway is at Havenstreet. The station buildings and platform were constructed by the Southern Railway in 1926...

Right:
...and incorporate a signalbox.

WAKEFIELD
CASTROL
MOTOR OIL
2
4

Left:
Across the line is the locomotive shed and coaling stage.

Right:
A water tower, transferred from Newport Station in 1971 is located alongside the Up platform. All trains in the Smallbrook direction take water here…

...before they depart.

A portrait of *Royal Engineer* on a light engine movement at Havenstreet.

The railway's other 1953 built Hunslet 0-6-0ST WD 198 *Waggoner* is captured coming off shed. Like *Royal Engineer* its ownership transferred to the IOWSR in 2008 having initially been on loan from the National Army Museum.

The station is a wonderful place to spend some time watching the locomotive movements…

SOUTHERN
FRESHWATER

Left:
...get up close and personal with the footplate...

Right:
...discovering the many railway-age artefacts performing the roles they were designed for...

...and marvelling at the wonderful restoration work on the wooden-bodied carriages, both externally. . .

...and internally.

The locomotive has a full head
of steam and the carriage
doors have been secured.

Left:
With a toot on his
whistle and a wave
of the green flag…

Right:
…the journey
can continue.

SOUTHERN
8

These two photographs date from July 1990 and show the 'Isle of Wight Railway' liveried *Newport* attacking the gradient away from Havenstreet en route to Wootton. The leading coach is IWR No.46 in its original teak finish. This coach had been a well-deserved winner of the Association of Railway Preservation Societies' award for best restored carriage.

11

Fenchurch and the four wheelers glide into Havenstreet.

Made famous by the Reverend Awdry as '*Stepney* the Bluebell Engine' No. 55 was built in 1875 and in its working life was particularly associated with the Hayling Island branch. It was sold to the Bluebell Railway in 1960, the first locomotive to be owned by them.

Newport climbs towards Briddlesford Bridge.

Beyond the bridge the line passes through Briddlesford Copse...

Left:
...and passed
Woodhouse Crossing.

Right:
An interesting feature of
the 'Terrier Gala' was
that the two visiting
locomotives faced
Smallbrook giving a
different perspective to
departures from
Wootton.

SOUTHERN
8
W 8

Left:
The more orthodox view of a Wootton to Havenstreet working.

Right:
Arrival at the western terminus. Hopefully the signalman is ready to receive the line token from the fireman.

One of my earliest visits to the IOWSR was in July 1990
during which I was fortunate to see No. 24 *Calbourne* at Wootton.

24
SOUTHERN
24

WOOTTON

The 1990 view of the station that had been completed by the preservation society four years earlier. The original Wootton Station, closed in 1953, was located in a cutting beyond the main road which is out of view behind and above the ticket office at the end of the line.

The society's re-creation of a small 'Victorian' island terminus is perfectly illustrated in this scene.

(Left) The signal box formerly performed the role at Newport and later Freshwater Stations until 1953 .*(Right)* By 2001 the ticket office, a nineteenth-century ticket collector's hut from Ryde Pier Head, had been relocated on the platform.

The train comes to a halt.

There is just time to inspect and photograph the locomotive before it is uncoupled to draw forward…

…prior to running round to prepare for the return journey.

A Victorian scene in all but fashion!

Having received the 'right-away' the return journey,
to Havenstreet and on to Smallbrook Junction, is underway.